First World War
and Army of Occupation
War Diary
France, Belgium and Germany

74 (YEOMANRY) DIVISION
229 Infantry Brigade
Devonshire Regiment
16th (Royal 1st Devon Yeomanry
and Royal North Devon Hussars) Battalion
1 May 1918 - 31 May 1919

WO95/3152/2

The Naval & Military Press Ltd
www.nmarchive.com
Published in association with The National Archives

Published by

The Naval & Military Press Ltd

Unit 10 Ridgewood Industrial Park,
Uckfield, East Sussex,
TN22 5QE England
Tel: +44 (0) 1825 749494

www.naval-military-press.com
www.nmarchive.com

Contents

Document type	Place/Title	Date From	Date To
Heading	WO95/3152/2 16 Battalion Devonshire Regiment		
Heading	74th Division 229th Infy Bde 16th Bn Devon Regt 1918 May-May 1919		
War Diary	On Bound H.M.T Leasowe Castle	01/05/1918	07/05/1918
War Diary	Rest Camp	08/05/1918	08/05/1918
War Diary	Marseilles	08/05/1918	08/05/1918
War Diary	On Train	09/05/1918	11/05/1918
War Diary	Favieres	12/05/1918	21/05/1918
War Diary	In Billets Sus Saint Leger	22/05/1918	24/05/1918
War Diary	Liencourt	25/05/1918	26/05/1918
War Diary	In Billets Liencourt	27/05/1918	30/05/1918
War Diary	Liencourt	31/05/1918	26/06/1918
War Diary	Witternesse	27/06/1918	30/06/1918
War Diary	Le Forest	01/07/1918	11/07/1918
War Diary	Guarbecque	12/07/1918	23/07/1918
War Diary	In The Line	24/07/1918	31/07/1918
War Diary	In The Field	01/08/1918	16/08/1918
War Diary	Ham En Artois	17/08/1918	31/08/1918
Miscellaneous	H.R.U 229 Bde	01/10/1918	01/10/1918
War Diary	Field	01/09/1918	30/09/1918
Miscellaneous	16th (Royal Devon Yeo) Bn Devon Regt Summary of Operation	12/09/1918	12/09/1918
Miscellaneous	16th (Royal Devon Yeo.) Bn Devon Regt	12/09/1918	12/09/1918
War Diary	Field	01/10/1918	30/11/1918
Heading	16th (Royal Devon Yeo.) Bn Devon Regt.		
War Diary	Field	01/12/1918	31/12/1918
War Diary	Field Grammont (Belgium)	01/01/1919	31/01/1919
War Diary	Grammont Belgium	01/02/1919	15/02/1919
War Diary	Grammont	16/02/1919	28/02/1919
War Diary	Grammont Belgium	01/03/1919	31/03/1919
War Diary	Grammont	01/04/1919	31/05/1919
Miscellaneous	H.Q 229 Bde	01/09/1918	01/09/1918

WO95/3152/2

16 Battalion Devonshire Repiment

74TH DIVISION

229TH INFY BDE

16TH BN DEVON REGT

1918 MAY - D~~EC 19~~18

~~JAN~~ - MAY 1919

16 Devon Rg

Vol 2

Instructions regarding War Diaries and Intelligence Summaries are contained in F. S. Regs., Part II. and the Staff Manual respectively. Title pages will be prepared in manuscript.

WAR DIARY
or
~~INTELLIGENCE~~ SUMMARY.
(Erase heading not required.)

Army Form C. 2118.

Place	Date	Hour	Summary of Events and Information	Remarks and references to Appendices
On Board H.M.T LEASOWE CASTLE	1/5/18		Bn on board H.M.T Leasowe Castle. (Sailed 1400)	
	2/5/18		" " " " " "	
"	3/5/18		" " " " " "	
	4/5/18		" " " " " "	
"	5/5/18		" " " " " "	
"	6/5/18		" " " " " "	
"	7/5/18	0900	Arrive at Marseilles	
		1400	Bn disembarks + marches to rest camp where the night is spent	
Rest Camp Marseilles	8/5/18	1100	Bn entrains at Marseilles, leave 1245	
On Train	9/5/18		" on train	
"	10/5/18		" " "	
"	11/5/18	0430	Arrive at NOYELLES, Bn detrains + marches to rest camp near NOYELLES	
		0915	Bn marches into billets at FAVIERES.	

Instructions regarding War Diaries and Intelligence Summaries are contained in F. S. Regs., Part II. and the Staff Manual respectively. Title pages will be prepared in manuscript.

WAR DIARY
or
~~INTELLIGENCE SUMMARY.~~
(Erase heading not required.)

Army Form C. 2118.

Place	Date	Hour	Summary of Events and Information	Remarks and references to Appendices
FAVIERES	12/5/18	0600	to 0630 Physical Drill	
		0800	" 1100 Company parades, Training of Specialists, Lectures	
		1400		
"	13/5/18	0600	to 0630 Physical "Drill"	
		0815	Bn Route march	
		1400	Company parades, Bombers (A Coy) under Lt Houghton	
"	14/5/18	0600	to 0630 Physical Drill	
		0830	to 1630 Gas Training carried out by Bn under the Training Staff of 7th Corp	
			Lt W.T.G. Kellock + 8 O.Rs. proceed to RUE on 2 days Gas course	
"	15/5/18	6.a.m.	to 6.30 a.m. Physical Drill + Bayonet fighting	
		8.a.m.	to 8-30.a.m. Gas Drill	
		10.a.m.	Bn marches to ST. FIRMANS to attend a lecture on B.F. + P.T. by Col Campbell	
"	16/5/18	6.a.m.	to 6-30 a.m. Physical Drill	
		8.a.m.	Company Training, B Coy Bombers under Lt Houghton	
		2.p.m.	" "	
			Major (A/Lieut Col) A.C. Mardon. R.N.D.H gazetted Lieut Colonel with precedence as from 6-11-17.	A.C.M.

Instructions regarding War Diaries and Intelligence Summaries are contained in F. S. Regs., Part II. and the Staff Manual respectively. Title pages will be prepared in manuscript.

WAR DIARY
or
~~INTELLIGENCE SUMMARY.~~
(Erase heading not required.)

Army Form C. 2118.

ROYAL DEVON YEOMANRY BN. DEVONSHIRE REGIMENT
No. ______
Date ______

Place	Date	Hour	Summary of Events and Information	Remarks and references to Appendices
FAVIERES	17/5/18	6.A.M.	Physical Drill	
		8-15.A.M.	Bn route march	
		2.P.M.	Company Training, C. Coy bombers under Lt Houghton	
"	18/5/18	8.A.M.	Bn marches to ground 2 miles W. of FAVIERES where Tactical exercise is carried out	
		7-30 P.M.	Bn marches to a field 200 yds E of E in ROMIOTTE & is given a "Gas Projector" demonstration	
			Appointments	
			Lieut W. T. G. Kellock appointed Gas officer	
			2/Lieut A. L. Houghton " Bombing "	
			345184 Cpl King " Sgt Drummer	
"	19/5/18		Sunday. Voluntary Service 11-A.M.	
			Holy Communion 11-30 "	
			Voluntary Service 5-45 P.M.	
			9. O Rs reported officially prisoners of war in Turkey.	
"	20/5/18	8.A.M.	Bn continues training in bayonet fighting & S.B.R. drill	
		3.15 P.M.	Bn less C. Coy marches to RUE & entrains	A.G.M.

D. D. & L., London, E.C. (A8093) Wt. W1771/M2031 750,000 5/17 Sch. 52 Forms C2118/14

Army Form C. 2118.

WAR DIARY
or
INTELLIGENCE SUMMARY.
(Erase heading not required.)

• Instructions regarding War Diaries and Intelligence Summaries are contained in F. S. Regs., Part II. and the Staff Manual respectively. Title pages will be prepared in manuscript.

Place	Date	Hour	Summary of Events and Information	Remarks and references to Appendices
	21/5/18	1 A.M.	Bn arrives at LIGNY ST. FOCHEL, detrain + march to SUS, SAINT, LEGER.	
		7 A.M.	C. Coy march to RUE + entrain	
		2. P.M.	C. Coy arrive at LIGNY, ST. FOCHEL, detrain + march to SUS, SAINT, LEGER where they join Bn.	
In billets SUS, SAINT, LEGER.	22/5/18	6. A.M.	Physical Drill	
		8. A.M.	Bn continues training, Specialists under Specialist Officers	
			New class of Lewis Gunners commences training under Lt Richardson	
"	23/5/18	6 A.M.	Physical Drill	
		8. A.M.	Training continued by Companies, Specialists under Specialist officers	
		2. P.M.	" " " " " " "	"
		3-45 P.M.	All Subaltern Officers instructed on Lewis Gun by Lt Richardson	
"	24/5/18	6. A.M.	Physical Drill	
		8. A.M.	Training continued by Companies, Specialists under Specialist officers	
		2. P.M.	" " " " " "	"
		3-45 P.M.	Subaltern Officers instruction on Lewis Gun continued	
LIENCOURT	25/5/18	8-45 A.M.	Bn marches to new billeting area in LIENCOURT.	
		3. P.M.	Subaltern Officers instruction on Lewis Gun	
"	26/5/18	10. A.M.	Inspection of billets by C.O	
		5. P.M.	Evening Service at LIENCOURT	R.S.M.

D. D. & L., London, E.C. (A8003) Wt. W1771/M2031 750,000 5/17 Sch. 52 Forms C2118/14

Instructions regarding War Diaries and Intelligence Summaries are contained in F. S. Regs., Part II. and the Staff Manual respectively. Title pages will be prepared in manuscript.

WAR DIARY
or
~~INTELLIGENCE SUMMARY.~~
(Erase heading not required.)

Army Form C. 2118.

Place	Date	Hour	Summary of Events and Information	Remarks and references to Appendices
In billets LIENCOURT	27/5/18	8.40 A.M.	Bn parade + inspection by G.O.C. 74th Division.	
		2.P.M.	Training by Companies continued	
		3.45 P.M.	Specialists under Specialist Officers. Subaltern Officers Lewis Gun course	
"	28/5/18	6.A.M.	Physical drill + bayonet fighting	
		8.A.M.	Training by Companies continued. Specialists under Specialist Officers	
		2.P.M.	Company parades for lectures etc	
		3.45 P.M.	Subaltern officers L.G. class. Lieut. W.R. Pettigrew appointed Bn Gas officer in place of Lt W.T.G. Hellock	
"	29/5/18	6 A.M.	Physical drill	
		8.A.M.	Training by Companies continued, Specialists under Specialist officers	
		2.P.M.	Lecture to Companies by Capt H.R. Fox + Capt A.W. Lewis on the Trenches	
		4.P.M.	Subaltern Officers L.G. class	
"	30/5/18	6 A.M.	Physical drill A. B. + C. Companies	
		7.45 A.M.	D. Coy shooting on range all day	
		8.A.M.	A. Coy + H. Qrs continue training	
		2.P.M.	B. + C. Companies training. A. B. + C. Companies have use of baths at BERLENCOURT during the day	

D. D. & L., London, E.C. (A8093) Wt. W1771/M2031 750,000 5/17 Sch. 52 Forms C2118/14

Instructions regarding War Diaries and Intelligence Summaries are contained in F. S. Regs., Part II. and the Staff Manual respectively. Title pages will be prepared in manuscript.

WAR DIARY
or
~~INTELLIGENCE SUMMARY.~~
(Erase heading not required.)

Army Form C. 2118.

Place	Date	Hour	Summary of Events and Information	Remarks and references to Appendices
LIENCOURT	31/5/18	6 A.M.	Physical drill + games	
		8 A.M.	Training by companies continued, bayonet fighting + S.B. Respirator drill practised. Specialists under Specialist Officers	
		10-30 A.M.	Subaltern officers Lewis Gun class	
		1 P.M.	Bn marches out to training ground South of LIENCOURT where a Tactical Scheme is carried out	
			The following officers joined the Bn during the month	
			Lieut W R Pettigrew 11th Devon Regt	
			2/Lt H. C. Eddington " "	
			2/Lt H. G. Eggins 2nd " "	
			2/Lt H. T. Hooper " "	
			Number of O.Rs joining Bn during the month 17.	
Awards.			345519 L/Cpl Percy W. awarded the CROIX DE GUERRE with permission to wear	

A. C. Mardon
Lt. Col. Comg.
Royal Devon Yeo Batt.
Devonshire Regt.

D. D. & L., London, E.C. (A8093) Wt. W1771/M2031 750,000 5/17 Sch. 52 Forms C2118/14

Instructions regarding War Diaries and Intelligence Summaries are contained in F. S. Regs., Part II. and the Staff Manual respectively. Title pages will be prepared in manuscript.

WAR DIARY
or
INTELLIGENCE SUMMARY.
(Erase heading not required.)

Army Form C. 2118.

16

DEVONSHIRE REGIMENT — Date June

Vol 3

Place	Date	Hour	Summary of Events and Information	Remarks and references to Appendices
LIENCOURT	1/6/18	6 am	Physical Drill & games	
		9.30 am	Bn. takes part in a Divisional Tactical exercise	
"	2/6/18		Sunday	
		11 am	Voluntary Service	
"	3/6/18	6 am	Physical Drill	
		8 am	Company Training by "C" & "D" Coys	
			"A" & "B" Coys. firing on Ranges all day	
		1.30 pm	Inspection of "D" in billets by M.O.	
		2 pm	Company Parades. "C" & "D" Coy Specialists under Specialist officers	
		4 pm	Subaltern officers' Lewis Gun Course continued	
			Lt. R. J. Lifter takes over duty of Adjutant vice Capt. R. G. Seymour who proceeds to staff duties of Bde H.Q.	
	4/6/18	6 am	Physical Drill	
		8 am	"A" "B" & "D" Coys. Company Training "C" Coy firing on Range	
		1.30 pm	Company Parades. Specialists under Specialist officers	
		5 pm	Subaltern Officers Lewis Gun Course continued	

E.P.S.

(A9175) Wt W2159/P364 600,000 12/17 D. D. & L. Sch. 52a. Forms/C2118/15

Instructions regarding War Diaries and Intelligence Summaries are contained in F. S. Regs., Part II. and the Staff Manual respectively. Title pages will be prepared in manuscript.

WAR DIARY
or
INTELLIGENCE SUMMARY.
(Erase heading not required.)

Army Form C. 2118.

Place	Date	Hour	Summary of Events and Information	Remarks and references to Appendices
LIENCOURT	5/6/18	6 am	Physical Drill & Games	
		8 am	Company Training "A" Coy on Range	
		11.30	Demonstration & Tactical Scheme with Tanks	
		2 pm	Company Parades. Specialists under Specialist officers	
		5 pm	Subaltern Officers Lewis Gun Course continued	
	6/6/18	6 am	Physical Training & Games	
		8 am	Coy Training. "B" Coy firing on Range	
		11.30	Tactical Scheme with Tanks by "A & D" Coys	
		2 pm	Coy Parades. Specialists under Specialist officers	
		5 pm	Subaltern Officers Lewis Gun Course continued	
	7/6/18	6 am	Physical Drill & Games	
		[illegible]	Battalion takes part in a Brigade Tactical Scheme	
		5 pm	Subaltern Officers Lewis Gun Course continued	
	8/6/18	6 am	Physical Drill & Games	
		8 am	3 Companies do Field Training. 1 Company on Range. Specialists under Specialist officers	
		2 pm	Company Parades. Specialists under Specialist officers	

M.H.S.

(A9175) W: W2358/P363 600,000 12/17 D. D. & L. Sch. 52a. Forms/C2118/15.

Instructions regarding War Diaries and Intelligence Summaries are contained in F. S. Regs., Part II. and the Staff Manual respectively. Title pages will be prepared in manuscript.

WAR DIARY
or
INTELLIGENCE SUMMARY.
(Erase heading not required.)

Army Form C. 2118.

ROYAL DEVON [illegible] BATTn. No.......... Date.......... DEVONSHIRE REGIMENT

Place	Date	Hour	Summary of Events and Information	Remarks and references to Appendices
LIENCOURT	8/6/18	5 p.m.	Subaltern Officers Lewis Gun Course continued	
	contd 9/6/18	a.m.	(Sunday) Voluntary Service [illegible]	
	10/6/18	6.0	Physical Drill & Games	
		9.0 a.m.	Company Training. Specialists under Specialists Officers	
			Fitting & testing in Gas chamber of Box Respirators	
		2.0 p.m.	Company Parade. Specialists under Specialist officers	
		5 p.m.	Subaltern officers Lewis Gun Course continued	
	11/6/18	6 a.m.	Physical Drill & Games.	
		9 a.m.	Company Training. [illegible] Company [illegible] with Tank	
			Specialists under Specialist Officers	
		2 p.m.	Company Parade. Specialists under Specialist officers	
		5 p.m.	Subaltern officers Lewis Gun Course continued	
	12/6/18	6 a.m.	Physical Training & Games	
		8 a.m.	Company Parades. Specialists under Specialist Officers	
		2 p.m.	Company Parades. Specialists under Specialist Officers	
	13/6/18	6 a.m.	Physical Training & Games	

(A9175) Wt W2358/P.63 600,000 12/17 D. D. & L. Sch. 52a. Forms/C2118/15

M.H.S.

Instructions regarding War Diaries and Intelligence Summaries are contained in F. S. Regs., Part II. and the Staff Manual respectively. Title pages will be prepared in manuscript.

WAR DIARY
or
INTELLIGENCE SUMMARY.
(Erase heading not required.)

Army Form C. 2118.

Place	Date	Hour	Summary of Events and Information	Remarks and references to Appendices
LIENCOURT	13/6/18	8.0 am	Company Training. Demonstration by Tanks with D Coy co-operating	
	(cont.)	1.0 pm	Signallers attend demonstration of Signalling with Contact aeroplanes	
		2.0 pm	Gas Demonstration by Divisional Gas Officer	
	14/6/18	6.0 am	Physical Training & Games.	
		8.0 am	Companies carry out Field Training. Specialists under Specialist Officers	
		2.0 pm	Company Parades. One company carries out practice in Clearing a Village. Specialists under Specialist Officers	
	15/6/18	6 am	Physical Training & Games	
		8.30 am	Inter-Brigade Scheme.	
	16/6/18	11	(Sunday) Voluntary Services	
	17/6/18	6 am	Physical Training or Games.	
		8.0 am	2 Companies do Company Training. 2 Companies fire on range. Specialists under specialist officers	
		2.0 pm	Company Parades. Specialists under specialist officers	
	18/6/18	6 am	Physical Drill or games	
		8.0 am	Company training. Specialists under specialist officers. Disinfection of clothing	
		2.0 pm	Company Parades. Specialists under specialist officers. Disinfection of clothing	

M.H.S.

Instructions regarding War Diaries and Intelligence Summaries are contained in F. S. Regs., Part II, and the Staff Manual respectively. Title pages will be prepared in manuscript.

WAR DIARY
or
INTELLIGENCE SUMMARY.
(Erase heading not required.)

Army Form C. 2118.

Place	Date	Hour	Summary of Events and Information	Remarks and references to Appendices
LIENCOURT	19.6.18	6 am	Physical Drill or games.	
		8.0 am	Disinfection of clothing for 2 companies. 2 companies Field Training. Specialists under specialist officers	
		2.0 pm	Company Parades, disinfection of clothing. Specialists under specialist officers	
	20.6.18	6 am	Physical Drill or games	
		8 am	Companies do Field training. Specialists under specialist officers	
		2 pm	Company Parades. Specialists under specialist officers.	
	21.6.18	6 am	Physical Drill or games	
		8 am	Companies carry out a tactical scheme. Specialists under specialist officers	
		2.0 pm	Company Parades. Specialists under specialist officers. Promulgation of sentence of F.G. Court Martial on 346106 Pte Thomas H, & 306077 Pte Murphy E.J.	
	22.6.18	6.0 am	Physical Drill or games	
		8.0 am	Battalion takes part in an inter-brigade scheme.	
	23.6.18	11.0 am	(Sunday) Voluntary Services	
	24.6.18	6.0 am	Physical Drill or games	

M.H.S.

Instructions regarding War Diaries and Intelligence Summaries are contained in F. S. Regs., Part II. and the Staff Manual respectively. Title pages will be prepared in manuscript.

WAR DIARY
or
INTELLIGENCE SUMMARY.
(Erase heading not required.)

ROYAL DEVON YEOMANRY BATTn. No.......... Date.......... DEVONSHIRE REGIMENT

Army Form C. 2118.

Place	Date	Hour	Summary of Events and Information	Remarks and references to Appendices
LIENCOURT	24/6/18	8.0 am	2 Coys Field Training 1 Coy fitting new respirators, 1 Coy on range	
			Specialists under specialist officers	
		2.0 pm	Company Parades; Specialists under specialist officers	
	25/6/18	6 am	Physical Drill & games	
		8.0 am	Company Parades Tank demonstration with 2 Coys co-operating	
			1 Coy fitting respirators & testing in chamber	
			Specialists under Specialist officers	
		2.0 pm	Company Parades Specialists under specialist officers	
	26/6/18	5 am	Battalion leaves area, marches to LIGNY FLOCHEL and thence by	
			rail to Aire, arriving WITTERNESSE 3 pm	
WITTERNESSE	27/6/18		During morning battalion engaged in tidying and cleaning billets	
		2.0 pm	Company Parades	
	28/6/18	6.0 am	Physical Drill	
		8 am	Company Parades Specialists under Specialist officers	
		2 pm	do do	
	29/6/18	8.30 am	Battalion proceed to new area at LE FORET arriving there 1.45 pm	
	30/6/18	8 am	2 Coys on trench digging working party	

W. H. Palmer Major Lt. Col. Comdg. Royal Devon Yeo. Batt. Devonshire Regt.

(A9175) Wt W2358/P360 600,000 12/17 D. D. & L. Sch. 52a. Forms/C2118/15

Instructions regarding War Diaries and Intelligence Summaries are contained in F. S. Regs., Part II, and the Staff Manual respectively. Title pages will be prepared in manuscript.

WAR DIARY
or
~~INTELLIGENCE SUMMARY.~~
(Erase heading not required.)

16 Devon

July -/18

Army Form C. 2118.

4

Place	Date	Hour	Summary of Events and Information	Remarks and references to Appendices
LE ECKET	1/7/18	8.30am	2 Companies on Working Parties. Signallers under Signalling Officer	
	2/7/18	8.30am	2 Companies on Working Party. Bathing parades during day under Company arrangements	
	3/7/18	8.am	2 Companies on Working Party. Scouts under Scout Officer. Reconnaissances of Battle Positions by Officers and NCOs not otherwise employed	
		7.15pm	2 Companies on Working Party.	
	4/7/18	8.am	2 Companies on Working Party. Scouts under Scout Officer. Reconnaissance of [illegible] STEENBECQUE line by all available officers & NCOs	
		[illegible]	2 Companies on Working Party.	
	5/7/18	8.am	2 Companies on Working Party. Scouts and Signallers under their own officers. Reconnaissance by available Officers & NCOs of defensive line	
		[illegible]	2 Companies on working party.	
	6/7/18	8.am	2 Companies on Working Party. Signallers under Signalling Officer	
		[illegible]	Inspection by Gas Officer under Company arrangement, of Box Respirators	
		[illegible]	Reconnaissance of defensive lines by available officers & N.C.Os	

(A9175) Wt W2153/P360 600,000 12/17 D. D. & L. Sch. 52a. Forms/C2118/15

Instructions regarding War Diaries and Intelligence Summaries are contained in F. S. Regs., Part II, and the Staff Manual respectively. Title pages will be prepared in manuscript.

WAR DIARY
or
~~INTELLIGENCE~~ SUMMARY.
(Erase heading not required.)

Army Form C. 2118.

Place	Date	Hour	Summary of Events and Information	Remarks and references to Appendices
LE ELRET	6/7/18	8.45 pm	2 Companies on Working Party	
	7/7/18	8 a.m	2 Companies on Working Party	
		8 a.m & pm	Box Respirator inspection by Gas Officer under Company arrangements	
			Reconnaissance of defensive lines by available officers & N.C.Os.	
		8.15 pm	4 Companies on Working Party	
		[illegible]	Voluntary Service (C of E)	
		7.45 pm	Holy Communion (C of E)	
	8/7/18	8 a.m	2 Companies on Working Party. Signallers under Signalling Officer	
			Scouts under Scout Officer. Reconnaissance of defensive lines by	
			available officers & N.C.Os. Inspection of Box Respirators by Gas Officer	
		8.45 pm	2 Companies on Working Party	
	9/7/18	8 a.m	2 Companies on Working Party. Specialists under Specialist Officers	
			Reconnaissance of defensive lines by available officers & N.C.Os.	
		8.45 pm	~~4~~ 2 Companies on Working Party	
	10/7/18	8 a.m	Specialists under Specialist Officers. Bathing under Company	
			arrangement during day.	[initials]

Instructions regarding War Diaries and Intelligence Summaries are contained in F. S. Regs., Part II. and the Staff Manual respectively. Title pages will be prepared in manuscript.

WAR DIARY
or
~~INTELLIGENCE~~ SUMMARY.
(Erase heading not required.)

Army Form C. 2118.

Place	Date	Hour	Summary of Events and Information	Remarks and references to Appendices
LE FORET	10/7/18	9. am	"B" Team proceeds to Divisional Reception Camp at WITTERNESSE	
	11/7/18	8.45am	Battalion move out to new billeting area at GUARBECQUE	
GUARBECQUE	12/7/18	8 am	Company Parades. Signallers under Signalling Officer	
		2 pm	do . do . do	
	13/7/18	8 am	do and Bathing. Specialists under Specialist Officers	
		2 pm	do . do . do . do.	
			Reconnaissance of defensive lines by officers NCOs & scouts	
	14/7/18	9.30	CO's inspection of billets	
			Divine Services Holy Communion 7.30 am Evening Service 5.30 pm Wesleyan - Nonconformists 11 am	
	15/7/18	8 am	One Company firing on range. Bathing during morning for 1 Company. Company Training. Inspection of Respirators by Bn Gas Officer. Specialists under specialist officers. Reconnaissance of defensive line.	
		2 pm	Company training & bathing. Specialists under specialist officers.	

(A9175) Wt W2353/P361 650,000 12/17 D. D. & L. Sch. 52a. Forms/C2118/15

Instructions regarding War Diaries and Intelligence Summaries are contained in F. S. Regs., Part II, and the Staff Manual respectively. Title pages will be prepared in manuscript.

WAR DIARY
or
~~INTELLIGENCE SUMMARY.~~
(Erase heading not required.)

ROYAL DEVON YEOMANRY BATTn. No. Army Form C. 2118. Date. DEVONSHIRE REGIMENT

Place	Date	Hour	Summary of Events and Information	Remarks and references to Appendices
GUARBECQUE	16/7/18	6 am	Physical Drill & Games	
		8 am	Company Parades, & Bathing. 1 Coy on range. Specialist Training	
GUARBECQUE		2 pm	do " " do " " do "	
	17/7/18	6 am	Physical Drill & Games	
		8 am	Company Parades. One Company on range. Specialists under specialist officers	
		2 pm	do " do " " do " do	
			Reconnaissance of defensive lines	
	18/7/18	6 am	Physical Drill & Games.	
		8 am	Company Parades. One Coy on range. Specialists under specialist officers	
		2 pm	do " do " " "	
			Reconnaissance of defensive lines.	
	19/7/18	6 am	Physical Drill & Games	
		8 am	Company Parades. 1 Company on range. Specialist Parades	
		2 pm	do " do " " do "	
	20/7/18	6 am	Physical Drill & Games	
		8 am	3 Coys Company Training 1 Coy on range " do	
		2 am	do Bathing & Parades. do " do	Gm

Instructions regarding War Diaries and Intelligence Summaries are contained in F. S. Regs., Part II, and the Staff Manual respectively. Title pages will be prepared in manuscript.

WAR DIARY
or
~~INTELLIGENCE SUMMARY~~.
(*Erase heading not required.*)

2118.

ROYAL DEVON YEOMANRY BATTn. No. .... Date .... DEVONSHIRE REGIMENT

Place	Date	Hour	Summary of Events and Information	Remarks and references to Appendices
1918	1918			
GUARBECQUE	21/7/18	6 am	Physical Drill & Games	
		8 am	Inspection of Box Respirators	
		7.30 am / 5.30 pm	Divine Services	
	22/7/18	8. am	Gas drill for all Companies. Specialist Training	
		2. pm	Company Parades " do "	
	23/7/18	6 am	Physical Drill & Games.	
		7 am	Inspection of Box Respirators	
		night 23/24th	Battalion take over portion of the line (AMUSOIRES-HAVERSKERQUE system between St Venant & Robecq)	
IN THE LINE	24/7/18	early morning	Considerable amount of shelling, HE & Gas during relief. ~~& [illegible]~~	
	25/7/18		A Raid was repulsed in early morning and about 20 casualties inflicted on enemy. Quiet during day. Work on improvement of position.	
	26/7/18		Battn holding the line. Conditions normal. Work on improving position	
	27/7/18		do do do do do do do	
	28/7/18		do do do do do do do	
	29/7/18		do do do do do do do	

(A9175) Wt W2355/P360 600,000 12/17 D. D. & L. Sch. 52a. Forms/C2118/15

Instructions regarding War Diaries and Intelligence Summaries are contained in F. S. Regs., Part II, and the Staff Manual respectively. Title pages will be prepared in manuscript.

WAR DIARY
or
~~INTELLIGENCE SUMMARY.~~
(Erase heading not required.)

Army Form C. 2118.

ROYAL DEVON YEOMANRY BATTn. No. .... Date .... DEVONSHIRE REGIMENT

Place	Date	Hour	Summary of Events and Information	Remarks and references to Appendices
IN THE LINE	30/7/18 31/7/18		Battalion hold line. Conditions normal. Work on improvement of position continues	

E. J. M. Holley [?] Capt for Lt. Col. Comg.
~~Royal~~ Devon Yeo. Batt.
Devonshire Regt.

(A9175) Wt W2355/P363 600,000 12/17 D. D. & L. Sch. 52a. Forms/C2118/15.

Instructions regarding War Diaries and Intelligence Summaries are contained in F. S. Regs., Part II, and the Staff Manual respectively. Title pages will be prepared in manuscript.

WAR DIARY
or
INTELLIGENCE SUMMARY.
(Erase heading not required.)

229/74

16 Devon

Army Form C. 2118.

5

Place	Date	Hour	Summary of Events and Information	Remarks and references to Appendices
IN THE FIELD	1/8/18		Battalion in front line of the AMUSOIRES - HAVERSKERQUE system (AMUSOIRES SECTOR). Conditions normal	
	2/8/18		ditto ditto	
	3/8/18		ditto ditto	
	4/8		ditto ditto	
	5/8		ditto ditto	
	6/8/18		As a result of a patrol report, enemy assumed to be withdrawing. One company following him up take 1 machine gun and one prisoner.	
	7/8/18		Contact by patrols kept with retiring enemy.	
	8/8/18		do do Battalion relieved in front line by 12th [illegible] and go into the Brigade Reserve.	
	9/8/18		Battalion in support. Working parties for improvement of line.	
	10/8/18		Battalion in support in new sector (ST FLORIS) east of ST VENANT	
	11/8/18		do ditto do	

(A9175) Wt W2358/P363 600,000 12/17 D. D. & L. Sch. 52a. Forms/C2118/15

Army Form C. 2118.

WAR DIARY
or
INTELLIGENCE SUMMARY.
(Erase heading not required.)

Instructions regarding War Diaries and Intelligence Summaries are contained in F. S. Regs., Part II, and the Staff Manual respectively. Title pages will be prepared in manuscript.

Place	Date	Hour	Summary of Events and Information	Remarks and references to Appendices
IN THE FIELD	[illegible]		[illegible] support in the ST FLORIS sector. Working parties improve defences	
	[illegible]		" do " do "	
	[illegible]		" do " do "	
	[illegible]		" do " do "	
	[illegible]		Battalion relieved by the [illegible]	
HAM EN ARTOIS	[illegible]		Battalion in billets at HAM EN ARTOIS	
		[illegible]	Company & specialist Parades.	
		[illegible]	do do	
	[illegible]	[illegible]	[illegible] Bathing	
	[illegible]	8 am	[illegible] the [illegible] health inspection by M.O.	
		2 pm	Battalion inspected by Brigade Commander	
	[illegible]	8 am	Company parades. Specialist Parades.	
		2 pm	do do	
	[illegible]	8 am	do do	
		2 pm	do do	
	[illegible]	8 am	do do Battalion Sports meeting during afternoon.	

Instructions regarding War Diaries and Intelligence Summaries are contained in F. S. Regs., Part II. and the Staff Manual respectively. Title pages will be prepared in manuscript.

WAR DIARY
or
INTELLIGENCE SUMMARY.
(Erase heading not required.)

Army Form C. 2118.

Place	Date	Hour	Summary of Events and Information	Remarks and references to Appendices
HAM EN ARTOIS	23/[illegible]	[illegible]	Company Parades. [illegible] Parades	
		2 pm	Lecture for all officers by Lt Col [illegible]	
			Company Parades	
	24/[illegible]	[illegible]	Battalion march out to relieve 1st KSLI in the left batt[n]	
			[illegible] of the line south of the LYS CANAL & EAST of CALONNE.	
			[illegible] made in [illegible] ASYLUM at ST VENANT for the day,	
			relief carried out after dark.	
	[illegible]		Battalion holding the line. Situation normal during the day,	
			[illegible]	
	[illegible]		Situation day & night normal	
	[illegible]		Situation normal. The [illegible] being relieved by the 57th	
			[illegible] battalion [illegible] relieved by [illegible] and return	
			to HAM EN ARTOIS [illegible]	
	[illegible]		[illegible]	
	[illegible]		Battalion entrain at BERGUETTE for CORBIE	
	30/[illegible]		Battalion arrive CORBIE and march to billets at FRANVILLERS.	
	31/[illegible]		Battalion move from billets in [illegible] and go into support of the line immediately north of PERONNE	

(A9175) Wt W2358/P560 600,000 12/17 D. D. & L. Sch. 52a. Forms/C2118/15.

To.
HQrs
229 Bde

Herewith copy of War Diary for the month of September 1918 please

R Cyples Capt. & Adjutant
Royal Devon Yeo. Batt
Devonshire Reg.

1/10/18

16th (Royal Devon Yeo.) Bn DEVON REGT.

Instructions regarding War Diaries and Intelligence Summaries are contained in F. S. Regs., Part II, and the Staff Manual respectively. Title pages will be prepared in manuscript.

WAR DIARY

or

~~INTELLIGENCE SUMMARY.~~

(Erase heading not required.)

Army Form C. 2118.

229
74
16 Devon R
Vol 6

Place	Date	Hour	Summary of Events and Information	Remarks and references to Appendices
Field	1st Sept 18	1 a.m	Bivouaced in neighbourhood of CLERY-SUR-SOMME. (3 p.m) Brigade Conference at 12th S.L.I. H.2. – plans for attack on 2nd (11 p.m) Relieved 2/2 LONDON REGT in support trenches in front of BOUCHAVESNES. BN H.2rs in ~~Old Quarry (C 20 c central)~~	
"	2/9/18	5.30 a.m	ZERO HOUR Attack on village of MOISLAINS. Strong resistance met with by A & B Companies – casualties heavy. CAPT. MUNTZ, 2/Lt MOODY, 2/Lt JONES, 2/Lt GARCIA wounded. Posts held by A Coy in MOISLAINS TRENCH. 2/Lt MORIARTY Gassed. D Coy relieved A & B Coys. BN H2rs situated C 22 central. Liason established on left with LONDON Rgt. Gas shelling at intervals throughout day – Heavy shelling during night 2nd/3rd. C Coy in support. 14 R[illegible] on right	See App. A/1
"	3/9/18		Position rearranged & consolidated. At Dusk gaps (untenable by day) occupied by C Company – continuous line with 47th DIV on left. Expected Counter attack undelivered.	
"	4/9/18	10 a.m	Patrol reports MOISLAINS evacuated by enemy. 2 p.m. Fighting Patrols pushed forward to obtain contact in cooperation with LONDONS & R.H. Lt EVANS Killed. C & D established line on canal bank in front of MOISLAINS. Village heavily shelled & gassed. 12 (midnight) Relieved by 24th LONDON. TOTAL Casualties 1st–4th 196 All ranks	196 All ranks
"	5/9/18		Bivouacked near CLERY. Capt Gyle returned from leave. Reinforcements 34/ors.	
"	6/9/18		Bn moved to Bivouac area in AIZECOURT. Bde in reserve. 2/Lt Johnson returned from leave.	
"	7/9/18		" " " " " LONGAVESNES & relieved 230th Bde. Bde in support	
"	8/9/18		Moved to neighbourhood of FAUSTINE QUARRY (Bn H2rs) Bde in support. Relief orders 12 midnight.	
"	9/9/18	4 a.m	Relieved 231 Bde in line. Intermittent shelling. 22 ors to U K leave	
"	10/9/18	4.30	ZERO HOUR Attack on TEA POST – met with strong resistance and counter attack. Withdrawal to original position, the captured position being untenable. 2/Lt WHICHER, 2/Lt BLICK wounded. 2/Lt Willoughby & 4 ors to UK leave. Reinforcements 2/Lt LESLIE + 22/ors	See Appx. B1
"	11/9/18		Relieved by 230th Bde. Bivouaced in neighbourhood of LONGAVESNES. Lieut Golding + 21 ors to UK leave	
"	12/9/18	3 p.m	Bn moved to TEMPLEUX-LA-FOSSE. Bde in Div Reserve. Total Casualties 8th to 10th 61 all ranks.	
"	13/9/18		Line of resistance reconnoitred. Company reorganisation. Enemy Air raid. Aeroplane brought down by A A	
"	14/9/18		Drill under Bn arrangement. Reconnaissance of main line carried out. Reinforcement 8 ors.	
"	15/9/18		Sunday. Divine Service 11.15 a.m & 6.0 p.m	

A.G.R.

(A9175) Wt W2358/P363 600,000 12/17 D. D. & L. Sch. 52a. Forms/C2118/15

Instructions regarding War Diaries and Intelligence Summaries are contained in F. S. Regs., Part II. and the Staff Manual respectively. Title pages will be prepared in manuscript.

WAR DIARY
or
~~INTELLIGENCE~~ SUMMARY.
(Erase heading not required.)

Army Form C. 2118.

Duplicate.

Place	Date	Hour	Summary of Events and Information	Remarks and references to Appendices
Field	16/9/18	1 pm	Lieut Machon, 2/Lieut Priestley, 2/Lieut Farrar joined Bn. Bn moved to forward area occupied by 230th Bde E of Longavesnes	
	17/9/18		Bn att to 231st Bde for coming operations. Relieved Bn in line. Bn HQrs at FAUSTINE QUARRY Operations normal	
	18/9/18	5.20 am	Zero Hour. All objectives reached many prisoners & guns captured. Another Bn leap frogged through the Bn remaining in support. Bn HQrs moved to ORCHARD POST	
			2/Lieut Farrar killed. Lieut Kellock & Lieut Machon wounded. 2/Lieut Leslie M.C. & 2/Lt Priestley wounded. 9 ORs returned from UK leave.	
	19/9/18		Bn returned to 229th Bde Command & on night 19th/20th moved to back area near FAUSTINE QUARRY 4 ORs returned from UK Leave. Lt Kevin-Yates & 2 ORs to UK Leave.	
	20/9/18	10 pm	Bn moved up into support line in front of RONSSOY. Bn HQrs located at ORCHARD POST	
	21/9/18		20 ORs returned from UK Leave Bn att to 231st Bde for coming operations & moved to position in BELLICOURT ROAD	
	22/9/18		Operations normal Lieut Houghton wounded. Lieut Wilkinson wounded	
	23/9/18		Bn reverted to command of BGC 229th Bde & moved to BENJAMIN POST – CAT POST Line 2/Lieut Carswell returned from Leave. Many patrols were done during night 23/24	
	24/9/18		Attack for zero hour 2.30 cancelled. Balloon Post pushed forward 250 yds in front of Bn. Lieut Richardson & Lieut Dickinson returned from Course. Relieved by 106th American Regt.	
	25/9/18		Bn bivouaced in neighbourhood of FAUSTINE QUARRY. Total casualties from 9/9/18–27/9/18 Bn entrained to billets near CORBIE. B Team rejoined. 5 Officers and 104 ORs 94 ORs	
	26/9/18		Lieut Cox, 2/Lieut Reed & 2/Lt SCHRADER joined Bn. Coys reorganised & refitted. 2 ORs to UK Leave	
	27/9/18	[illegible] pm	Lieut Montgomery & 28 ORs to UK Leave Bn entrained at MERICOURT L'ABBE for BERGUETTE. 'C' Coy acted as Loading Party to Bn	
	28/9/18	10 am	Arrived BERGUETTE. Moved to Billets in HAM-EN-ARTOIS 'B' Coy acted as unloading party to Bde. Lieut Willoughby returned from leave	
	29/9/18	12 noon	Sunday. Divine Service 9 am & 6.30 pm. Reinforcements from UK 88 ORs COs Conference	
	30/9/18	8 am 11 am	Coy Parades. Lieut Brimsbire MC returned from Hospital. Reinforcements 2/Lieut SHAMBROOK " Golding " " Leave & 20 ORs joined Bn.	

A. C. Mardon Lt. Col. Comg.
Royal Devon Yeo. Batt.
Devonshire Regt.

(A9175) W: W2355/P363 6,0,000 12/17 D. D. & L. Sch. 52a. Forms/C2118/15

Appendix A

A

16th (Royal Devon Yeo.) Bn DEVON REGT.

Summary of Operations 2nd Sept 18

The task allotted to the Battn for the attack on 2nd Sept 18 was to support the [illegible] in the advance. Two Companies (A & B) were to clear up the village of MOISLAINS (reported to be evacuated by the enemy) and afterwards as quickly as possible resume their position with the remaining Companies in support. The intended manoeuvre to be carried out by one of the leading Bns was not successful owing to the enemy holding MOISLAINS in force and catching them in enfilade. A & B Coys developed an attack against the village with both flanks open. Heavy casualties ensued from shell & M.G. fire and only [illegible] were taken. At dusk A & B Companies [illegible] to their position leaving forward posts in MOISLAINS [illegible] these afterwards relieved by D Coy. The position held were approximately [illegible] [illegible] Eastern [illegible] until evacuation of MOISLAINS by the enemy on 4.9.18.

P.T.O.

APPENDIX. B.

16th (Royal Devon Yeo.) Bn DEVON REGT.

Summary of Operations 9th Sept 18 – 12th Sept 18

During the night of the 9th/10th and morning of the 10th September, the Brigade carried out an attack on the high ground running from St Emilie to Ronssoy thence S.W. The greater part of this objective was taken by the 16th Devons and 14th RL Highlrs but the retention of this ground was contingent on the capture of EPEHY which wasn't successful with the result that by 9 p.m. we had given up TEA POST, the last hold we had on high ground & withdrawn to our original line. Heavy casualties were suffered and the Bde were relieved that night.

OCTOBER [illegible]

Army Form C. 2118.

Instructions regarding War Diaries and Intelligence Summaries are contained in F. S. Regs., Part II, and the Staff Manual respectively. Title pages will be prepared in manuscript.

WAR DIARY
16th (Royal Devon Yeo.) Bn DEVON REGT.

~~INTELLIGENCE SUMMARY.~~ 16th (Royal Devon Yeo.) Bn DEVON REGT.

(Erase heading not required.)

V 7

Place	Date	Hour	Summary of Events and Information	Remarks and references to Appendices
Field.	1st OCTOBER 1918	8-11	Coy Parades. Training of Signallers & Lewis Gunners. S.B.R's inspected by Gas Officer. 7 ors. to hospital. Capt FEHILY to UK leave. Lieut G BENET M.C. U.S.A. joined Battn.	
"	2/10/18	10.30	Bn moved via BURBURE to HINGES. Bde in Reserve. Lt Col AE MARDON to hospital. Capt J.F. Shelley to Bn. Command.	
"	3/10/18	8-11	Coy Parades. Lewis Gunners & Signallers training. 20 ors. to UK. Leave. Reinforcements 30 ors joined Bn & 21 ors returned from UK leave. Bn moved to RICHEBOURG D'AVOUE.	4.30pm
"	4/10/18	7 a.m.	Lieut SR FARNSWORTH & 20 ors to UK. Leave. 8 ors to ex-Regtl employ. Bn moved to HERLES.	
"	5/10/18	8-11	Lieut JEH DUCKWORTH to Course. Lieut Golding to UK. Coy Parades. Training of Signallers & Lewis Gunners.	
"	6/10/18	9-11	New Lewis Gunner training. Sunday. Divine Services {11 a.m. 5.30 p.m.} Reinforcements arrived {1 o.r. 3 ors from UK leave, 18 ors from Hospital}	
"	7/10/18	1-5 pm	Batt [illegible] night in trenches at RICHEBOURG. CAPT J.F. SHELLEY [illegible] Reception Camp. CAPT. E.J.H. [illegible] M.C. took over command of the Battalion.	
"	8/10/18	7 a.m.	Batt. [illegible] L'AVENTURE. Bde in reserve. Batt. billets in German [illegible]	
"	9/10/18	8-11	Specialist & company training. [illegible] N.E. of [illegible] Corps Line of Resistance.	
"	[illegible]	[illegible]	Specialists [illegible]. Batt. [illegible] N.30.d & 0.25.c.	{2/Lt. [illegible] 2/Lt [illegible] 2/Lt MACKINTOSH 2/Lt BROWN 2/Lt CHANIN [illegible] Battn.} 2/Lt GENT.
"	[illegible]	[illegible]	Batt. [illegible] line [illegible] (Trenches) [illegible] Corps Line of Resistance.	
"	[illegible]	[illegible]	Batt. [illegible] Corps Line of Resistance.	
"	13/10/18	[illegible]	Batt. [illegible] (HERLIES) & [illegible] concrete dug-outs. [illegible] on Corps Line	
"	14/10/18	[illegible]	[illegible] Resistance.	
"	15/10/18	[illegible]	Batt. moved [illegible] support at PETIT HAUBOURDIN.	
"	16/10/18	6 a.m.	[illegible] HAUBOURDIN. Batt in support. [illegible] Batt. [illegible] support [illegible]	[illegible] all night
"				

Instructions regarding War Diaries and Intelligence Summaries are contained in F. S. Regs., Part II. and the Staff Manual respectively. Title pages will be prepared in manuscript.

WAR DIARY

Army Form C. 2118.

~~16th (Royal Devon Yeo.) Bn DEVON REGT.~~ or ~~INTELLIGENCE SUMMARY~~. 16th (Royal Devon Yeo.) Bn DEVON REGT.

(Erase heading not required.)

Place	Date	Hour	Summary of Events and Information	Remarks and references to Appendices
Field	17/10/18	5 a.m. 6.30	Patrols [illegible] HAUBOURDIN [illegible] outskirts of LILLE. [illegible] LILLE evacuated. [illegible] HAUT DEULE CANAL. Pontoon bridges [illegible] Canal	
			[illegible] p.m. [illegible] GRANDE RONCHIN [illegible] 11 p.m. [illegible] line of [illegible]	
"	[illegible]		[illegible] GRANDE RONCHIN	
			[illegible] Brigade. Enemy encountered in neighbourhood of	
			[illegible] resistance [illegible] Railway embankment.	
"			[illegible] Railway. A C & D. Coys in front line. A & B. in support.	
			[illegible] 2 a.m. Casualties [illegible] wounded. [illegible] all night.	
			[illegible] enemy. [illegible] N. 16. central to N. 28. central. East of [illegible]	
			[illegible] M. 36. central. [illegible]	
			[illegible] position [illegible] ground	
			[illegible]	
			[illegible] Billets at SIN [illegible]	
			[illegible] N. 13. central – N. 25. central	
			[illegible] BASIEUX [illegible] Billets for night	
			B [illegible]	
			L'EPINE – Billets.	
			[illegible] MARQUAIN [illegible] Billets.	
			[illegible]	
			[illegible]	
			[illegible] training [illegible] continued.	
			[illegible]	
			[illegible] 230th Bde. [illegible] BAISIEUX.	
	27/10		[illegible]	
	28/10		[illegible]	

(A9173) Wt W2358/P36 600,000 12/17 D. D. & L. Sch. 52a. Forms/C2118/15

Instructions regarding War Diaries and Intelligence Summaries are contained in F. S. Regs., Part II. and the Staff Manual respectively. Title pages will be prepared in manuscript.

WAR DIARY
or
~~INTELLIGENCE SUMMARY.~~
(Erase heading not required.)

Army Form C. 2118.

16th (Royal Devon Yeo.) Bn DEVON REGT.

Place	Date	Hour	Summary of Events and Information	Remarks and references to Appendices
Field	27/10/18	9-30	Church Parade in field [illegible] Wearing mill. Capt. [illegible] rejoins Battn from leave & takes over duties of Adjutant - as	from 28.10.18.
"	28/10/18	8.30 2.30	Training continued. Capt. [illegible] relinquishes Adjutancy & takes command of C. Coy. Lt. REED, takes over duties of Asst Adjt.	
"	29/10/18	8.30 2.30	Training continued. A.B. & [illegible] Coys attend bathing parade. [illegible] Lt. WILLIAMSON 10 O.R. to U.K. - struck off strength. 19 O.R. returned from leave.	[illegible] BAISIEUX
"		9.30 pm	BAISIEUX shelled intermittently for half an hour. 1 O.R. wounded.	
"	30/10/18	8.30 2.30 10.0-11	Training continued under Coy arrangements. C & D. Coys attend bathing parade. BAISIEUX [illegible] BAISIEUX [illegible]. Lt. DUCKWORTH returned from Course. 30x rifle range dug by B. Coy [illegible]. No casualties.	7 O.R. rejoined from leave. 2 O.R. rejoined from [illegible]. 1 O.R. from Hospl.
"	31/10/18	8.30 2.30	Training continued under Company arrangements. [illegible] {B. Coy used range 9-11-30. {A Coy " " 2-3-30.	

E. J. H. [illegible]
Capt.
~~Lt. Col.~~ Comg.
Royal Devon Yeo. Batt.
Devonshire Regt.
31/10/18.

(A9175) Wt W2358/P361 600,000 12/17 D. D. & L. Sch. 52a. Forms/C2118/15.

229/74

Army Form C. 2118.

Instructions regarding War Diaries and Intelligence Summaries are contained in F. S. Regs., Part II. and the Staff Manual respectively. Title pages will be prepared in manuscript.

WAR DIARY

or

~~INTELLIGENCE SUMMARY~~. 10th (Royal Devon Yeo.) Bn. DEVON REGT.

(Erase heading not required.)

Vol 8

Place	Date	Hour	Summary of Events and Information	Remarks and references to Appendices
[illegible]	[illegible]	[illegible]	[illegible]	[illegible]

[illegible]

Instructions regarding War Diaries and Intelligence Summaries are contained in F. S. Regs., Part II, and the Staff Manual respectively. Title pages will be prepared in manuscript.

WAR DIARY
or
~~INTELLIGENCE SUMMARY~~. 16th (Royal Devon Yeo.) Bn DEVON REGT.

(Erase heading not required.)

Army Form C. 2118.

Place	Date	Hour	Summary of Events and Information	Remarks and references to Appendices
[illegible]	[illegible]/11/18	8 Am.	[illegible] stood by in billets awaiting order to practice the manning of Battle positions	
		9 A.m.	[illegible] to man Battle positions	
	[illegible]	[illegible]	[illegible]	[illegible] Area.
	[illegible]	9 Am.	[illegible] of Battalion by Commanding Officer.	
		[illegible]	[illegible] STOQUET [illegible]	
	[illegible]	[illegible]	[illegible] to BOURGHAL [illegible]	[illegible]
	[illegible]	[illegible]	[illegible] to PIPAIX [illegible]	
	[illegible]	7.30	[illegible] O.R. [illegible] engaged on Railway Work on main TOURNAI Line.	
		[illegible]	[illegible] Battalion at PIPAIX.	
	[illegible]/11/18	7.15	A & B Companies [illegible] engaged on Railway Work on main TOURNAI Line.	
		[illegible]	[illegible]	
		[illegible]	[illegible] LEUZE.	
	[illegible]/11/18	[illegible]	[illegible] 6 officers engaged on Railway Work on main TOURNAI Line.	9 O.R. rejoined Batt.
	"	[illegible]	A & B [illegible]	2 O.R. joined as Reinforcements
		[illegible]	[illegible]	
	[illegible]	[illegible]	A & B [illegible] work [illegible]	2/Lt. [illegible] EVANS & 20 O.R. rejoined [illegible] R.E.s
	[illegible]	[illegible]	[illegible]	2/Lt. GRANGER BROWN + 16 O.R. rejoined Batt. from Courses [illegible]
		[illegible]	[illegible]	
"	24/11/18	9 Am.	A & B Coys engaged on Railway Work on main Tournai Line.	Lt. J.F.W. CARSWELL [illegible]
			[illegible] at PIPAIX for C & D Coys.	2/Lt. GRANGER BROWN appointed Intelligence Officer.

(A9175) Wt W2358/P360 600,000 12/17 D. D. & L. Sch. 52a. Forms/C2118/15

407

Instructions regarding War Diaries and Intelligence Summaries are contained in F. S. Regs., Part II. and the Staff Manual respectively. Title pages will be prepared in manuscript.

WAR DIARY
or
~~INTELLIGENCE SUMMARY.~~ 16th (Royal Devon Yeo.) Bn DEVON REGT.

(Erase heading not required.)

Army Form C. 2118.

Place	Date	Hour	Summary of Events and Information	Remarks and references to Appendices
Field	25/11/18.	7.15 am – 11 am	A & B Coy. engaged on Railway – main TOURNAI Line.	9 O.R. rejoined Batt. from hospital.
"	"	[illegible]	C & D Coys. Company Parades & Training.	
"	26/11/18	7.15 am	[illegible] & Training as for 25/11/1918.	
"	27/11/18	7.15	[illegible] & Training as for 25/11/18 – except C & D Coys – Railway Work; A & B Coys – Training.	
"	28/11/18	7.45 – 11 am	Railway Work carried out by Battalion less Specialists & [illegible].	
"	"	2 pm – 3 pm	Concert at LEUZE for Battalion. Lt Col. E.G. HOLLEY M.C. proceeded to U.K on 14 days leave. Capt. H.R. FOX. M.C. took over the Command of the Battalion.	
"	29/11/18	[illegible] – 11 am	Railway Work carried out by C & D Company.	2/Lt W.G. [illegible] rejoined from special leave.
"	"		[illegible] & Training under Company arrangements.	
"	30/11/18		Railway Work carried out by A & B Coys on main TOURNAI LINE.	
"	"		Training under Company arrangements carried out by C & D Coys.	

H.R. Fox Capt ~~Lt.Col.~~ Comg.
Royal Devon Yeo. Batt.
Devonshire Regt.

1st Dec 1918.

16th (Royal Devon Yeo.) Bn DEVON REGT.

To H.Q.

229th Bde.

Herewith War Diary

for December. 1918.

[illegible]

[illegible]

~~Capt. &~~ Adjutant

Royal Devon Yeo.

Devonshire R[illegible]

2/1/19.

Instructions regarding War Diaries and Intelligence Summaries are contained in F. S. Regs., Part II. and the Staff Manual respectively. Title pages will be prepared in manuscript.

Dec/18

V 8 9

Army Form C. 2118.

WAR DIARY
or
~~INTELLIGENCE SUMMARY.~~ 16th (Royal Devon Yeo.) Bn DEVON REGT.

(Erase heading not required.)

Place	Date	Hour	Summary of Events and Information	Remarks and references to Appendices
Fil[illegible]	1/12/18	7.45	"C" & "D" Coys carried out Railway Work on main TOURNAI Line. 2/Lt. L. T. MANSON joined Batt. as reinforcement.	
		[illegible] 10.45	Battalion less C & D Coys attended Church Parade in [illegible] PIPAIX.	
"	[illegible]	7.45	A & B Coys. Railway Work. "C & D" Coys. Parade under Company arrangements. [illegible] C & D [illegible] Bath at LEUZE.	
"	3/12/18	7.45	C & D Coys. Railway Work. A & B Coys. Bath at LEUZE. A & B Coys. Lecture by Divisional Educational Officer.	
"	[illegible]		Holiday for FOOTBALL Competition.	
"	[illegible]	7.45	A & B Coys. - Railway Work.	
"		[illegible]	[illegible] Coys. Parade under [illegible]. [illegible] Recreational Training. Lt. Col. A. C. MARNDON. D.S.O. returned from U.K. and resumed command of Battalion.	
"	6/12/18	7.45	C & D Coys. - Railway Work.	
"		[illegible]	[illegible] & Recreational Training under Coy arrangements.	
	7/12/18	[illegible]	Battalion [illegible] to BARRY (main LEUZE - TOURNAI road.) for visit [illegible] H.M. THE KING.	
	8/12/18	7.45 [illegible]	~~A & B Coys. - Railway Work~~	
"		9.30 am.	[illegible] Parade in [illegible], PIPAIX ~~for~~ ABC Battalion [illegible]. Lt. [illegible] D. A. Falcon joined Battalion as reinforcements.	
	9/12/18	7.45 [illegible]	A & B Coys. - Railway Work.	
		[illegible] 30	C & D [illegible] Company Parades & Recreational Training under Company Arrangements.	
	10/12/18	[illegible]	[illegible] Battalion under Company arrangements.	
	11/12/18	7.45 am 4 pm	C & D Company. - Railway Work.	A. [illegible]

(A9125) Wt W2358/P363 600,000 12/17 D. D. & L. Sch. 52a. Forms/C2118/15

Instructions regarding War Diaries and Intelligence Summaries are contained in F. S. Regs., Part II, and the Staff Manual respectively. Title pages will be prepared in manuscript.

WAR DIARY
or
~~INTELLIGENCE SUMMARY~~ 16th (Royal Devon Yeo.) Bn DEVON REGT.

(Erase heading not required.)

Army Form C. 2118.

Place	Date	Hour	Summary of Events and Information	Remarks and references to Appendices
Field	11/12/18	8.30 – 10.30	A & B. Coys. Company Parades.	
"	"	3 pm – 5 pm	A & B Coys attended BATHS AT LEUZE.	
"	12/12/18	8 AM – Noon	A & B. Coys – Railway Work. C & D Coys attended baths at LEUZE.	
"	"	9 A.M. – [illegible]	C & D. Coy. – Parade under Company arrangements.	
"	"	2 pm – 4 pm	Recreational & Educational Training for Battalion.	
"	13/12/18	8 AM – Noon; 2.30 – 4 pm	C & D. Coys – Railway Work. A & B. Cy parades & Educational & Recreational training.	
"	14/12/18	8 AM – 2 pm; 8.30 – 4 pm	A & B. Coys. Railway Work. C & D. Coy Parades, Educational & Recreational training.	
"	15/12/18	7.15 AM	Battalion moved to OEUDEGHIEM & billeted there the night of 15/16 DEC. 1918.	
"	16/12/18	8.45 AM	Battalion moved to GRAMMONT & billeted there.	
"	17/12/18	8 [illegible] – 4 [illegible]	Parades & Work. Recreational & Educational training under Company arrangements.	
"	18/12/18	[illegible]	As for 17/12/18.	
"	19/12/18	[illegible]	As for 17/12/18.	
"	20/12/18	8.30 AM	[illegible] Parades. Educational & Recreational training all under Company arrangements.	
"	21/12/18	8.30 – 12.0	[illegible] march for Battalion. Recreation during afternoon.	
"	22/12/18	11 AM	Church Parade for Battalion.	
"	23/12/18	8.30 – 4 pm	Parades under Company arrangements. Recreational Training.	[illegible]

(A9175) Wt W2358/P360 600,000 12/17 D. D. & L. Sch. 52a. Forms/C2118/15

Instructions regarding War Diaries and Intelligence Summaries are contained in F. S. Regs., Part II, and the Staff Manual respectively. Title pages will be prepared in manuscript.

WAR DIARY

or

~~INTELLIGENCE SUMMARY~~. 16th (Royal Devon Yeo.) Bn DEVON REGT.

(Erase heading not required.)

Army Form C. 2118.

Place	Date	Hour	Summary of Events and Information	Remarks and references to Appendices
Field	24/12/18	8.30. 4.pm.	Parades under Company arrangements. Recreational Training.	
"	25/12/18		Xmas Day. Parades NIL.	
"	26/12/18		Holiday.	
"	27/12/18	9.0 12.0 2-4	Parades & Educational Training under Company arrangements Recreational Training.	
"	28/12/18	9.0 12.0	Parades & Educational Training under Company arrangements.	
"	29/12/18	10.0 11.30	Parade Service in Recreation Room. St Catharine's College. GRAMMONT.	
"	30/12/18	8-0 3.30	BATHS AT GRAMMONT for BATTALION. PARADES & EDUCATIONAL TRAINING UNDER COMPANY ARRANGEMENTS.	
"	31/12/18	8-0 3.30	Parades & Educational Training under Company arrangements.	

31/12/1918

[illegible signature]
Lt. Col. Comg.
Royal Devon Yeo. Batt.
Devonshire Regt.

4

Jan 1919

Instructions regarding War Diaries and Intelligence Summaries are contained in F. S. Regs., Part II. and the Staff Manual respectively. Title pages will be prepared in manuscript.

WAR DIARY
or
~~INTELLIGENCE SUMMARY.~~
(Erase heading not required.)

16th (Royal Devon Yeo.) Bn DEVON REGT.

Army Form C. 2118.

VIII 10

Place	Date	Hour	Summary of Events and Information	Remarks and references to Appendices
[illegible] Grammont	1/1/19	-	Holiday.	
"	2/1/19	[illegible]	Parades under Company arrangements & Educational Training; Recreational Training.	
"	3/1/19	9-10.30 / 2.30-4pm	Route march along Canal Bank to Grammont outskirts. Educational & Recreational Training.	
"	4/1/19	8.30 / 12-0	Parades under Company arrangements.	
"	5/1/19	9 AM / 10 30 pm	PARADE SERVICE IN RECREATION ROOM. RUE DE COLLEGE GRAMMONT. COL. A. C. MARDON. D.S.O. proceeded U.K. on 14 days spec. leave. Major E. J. H. Holley M.C. assumed command of Battalion	
"	6/1/19	9-12 / 2-4	Parades under Coy arrangements. & Educational Training. Recreational Training.	
"	7/1/19	9.30 / 12-0	Presentation of Ribbons to 229 Brigade in Square at Grammont. Parades under Company arrangements	
"	"	2-0 / 4-0	Recreational Training	
"	8/1/19	9-10.30 am / [illegible]	Parades under company arrangements. Medical Officer inspects all men in battalion by companies.	
"	"	11-12 / 2-4	Educational Training. Recreational Training	
"	9/1/19	9-12.30 / 2-4	Parades under company arrangements [illegible] Recreational Training	
"	10/1/19	9-10.30 / 11-12 / 2-4	Parades under company arrangements. Educational Training. Recreational Training	
"	11/1/19	9-11 / 2-4	Battalion Route March. Recreational Training	
"	12/1/19	9.45	Parade service for battalion	
"	13/1/19	9-10.30 / 11-12 / 2-4	Parades under company arrangements. Educational Training. Recreational Training	
"	14/1/19	9-12.30 / 2-4	Battn route march [illegible] for men as detail. Cross country run for any [illegible] wishes to volunteer. Recreational Training	

(A9175) Wt W2358/P360 600,000 12/17 D. D. & L. Sch. 52a. Forms/C2118/15

Instructions regarding War Diaries and Intelligence Summaries are contained in F. S. Regs., Part II, and the Staff Manual respectively. Title pages will be prepared in manuscript.

WAR DIARY

or

~~INTELLIGENCE SUMMARY.~~ 16th (Royal Devon Yeo.) Bn DEVON REGT.

(Erase heading not required.)

Army Form C. 2118.

Place	Date	Hour	Summary of Events and Information	Remarks and references to Appendices
In the Field		9-10.30	Company parades for H.Q., C & D Companies	
Grammont	15/1/19	8.30-12	A, B & half Transport have the use of battalion baths	
(Belgium)	"	1-3.30	C Co & half Transport have the use of battalion baths	
		11-12	Educational training for companies not using baths. Afternoon. Recreational training	
"	16	8.30-10.30	D Co have use of baths	
		9-10	A B & C Co Educational training	
"		10-12.30	Transport will use baths	
		1.30-4	Headquarters use baths	
"	17	9-10.30	Parades under company arrangements	
"		11-12	Educational training Afternoon Recreational training	
"	18	9-10.30	Parade under company arrangement	
		10 AM	Commanding Officer inspect A & D Co billets	
"		11-12	Educational training	
"		2-4	Recreational training	
"	19	9.30	Church parade	
	20	9 AM	Party detailed for review at Brussels practice Ceremonial parade.	
		9-10.30	Remainder of companies under company arrangements	
		11-12	Educational training	
		2-4	Recreational training	
	21	8.30 AM	Composite Co for march past at Brussels inspected by B.G.C.	
		9-10.30	Remainder of companies under company arrangements.	
		11-12	Educational training	
		2-4	Recreational training	
		9.30	The Commanding Officer to inspect Composite Company selected for the review at Brussels	
	22	9-10	Remainder of Coys parade under company arrangements	
		11-12	Educational training	
		2-4	Recreational training	
	23	9.30	Inspection of Composite Company by C.O.	
		9-10.30	Remainder of battalion under company arrangements	
		11-12	Educational training	
		2-4	Recreational training	

Instructions regarding War Diaries and Intelligence Summaries are contained in F. S. Regs., Part II, and the Staff Manual respectively. Title pages will be prepared in manuscript.

WAR DIARY
or
~~INTELLIGENCE SUMMARY.~~
(Erase heading not required.)

Army Form C. 2118.

16th (Royal Devon Yeo.) Bn DEVON REGT.

Place	Date	Hour	Summary of Events and Information	Remarks and references to Appendices
Field (GRAMMONT BELGIUM)		8-20	Composite company for ~~review~~ at Brussells inspected by B G C	
	24	9-10.30	Remainder of battalion under company arrangements.	
		11-12	Educational training	
		2-4	Recreational training	
"		7.AM	The composite company parade for entraining & proceed to Brussells.	
	25	9-10.30	Remainder of battalion under company arrangements.	
		11-12	Educational training	
"		2-4	Recreational training	
	26		9.00 Church parade	
	27	9-10.30	Parades under company arrangements	
		11-12	Educational training	
		2-4	Recreational training	
"	28	9-10.30	Parades under company arrangements	
		11-12	Educational training	
		2-4	Recreational training	
"	29	9-10.30	Parades under company arrangements	
		9.30-10.30	Medical Officers inspection of the battalion	
		11-12	Educational training	
		2-4	Recreational training	
	30	9-10	Company Parades.	
		11-12	Lecture by Major Beckett M C (R F.A) on Formation of German Empire in Europe	
	31	2-4	Recreational Training	
		9-12	[illegible] for 30/1/19.	

E. J. Y. [illegible] Major Comg. Royal Devon Yeo. Batt. Devonshire Regt.

1/2/1919

(A9175) Wt W2358/P36 · 600,000 12/17 D. D. & L. Sch. 52a. Forms/C2118/15

16 Devons

Army Form C. 2118.

WAR DIARY
or
~~INTELLIGENCE SUMMARY.~~
(*Erase heading not required.*)

Instructions regarding War Diaries and Intelligence Summaries are contained in F. S. Regs., Part II, and the Staff Manual respectively. Title pages will be prepared in manuscript.

Vol 11

Place	Date	Hour	Summary of Events and Information	Remarks and references to Appendices
[illegible] Belgium	1/2/19	9-10	Company Parades	
	1/2/19	10-12	Educational Training	
"		2-4	Baths & Recreational Training.	
"	2.2.19	9.45	Church Parade in Recreation Room. 24 O.R. proceeded U.K. for demobilization	
	3.2.19	9-4	Company Parades. Educational & Recreational Training.	
	4.2.19	[illegible]	Parade for Battalion at [illegible]	
	5.2.19	9-4	Company Parades. Educational & Recreational Training. 6 O.R. proceeded U.K. for demobilization.	
	6.2.19	9-4	Company Parades. Educational & Recreational Training. 4 O.R. proceeded U.K. for demobilization	
	7.2.19	[illegible]	Company Parades. Educational & Recreational Training. 2/Lt. W.G. WARWICK & 4 O.R. proceeded U.K. for demobilization.	
	8.2.19	[illegible]	Company Parades. Educational & Recreational Training. [illegible] + 52 O.R. proceeded U.K. for demobilization.	
	9.2.19	9.45	Church Parade in Recreation Room. 46 O.R. proceeded U.K. for demobilization.	
"	10.2.19	9-4	Company Parades. Educational & Recreational Training	
"	11.2.19	9-4	Do Do	
"	12.2.19	9-4	Do Do	
"	13.2.19	9-4	Do Do	
"	14.2.19	9-4	Do Do	
"	15.2.19	9-4	Do Do.	

Instructions regarding War Diaries and Intelligence Summaries are contained in F. S. Regs., Part II, and the Staff Manual respectively. Title pages will be prepared in manuscript.

WAR DIARY

or

~~INTELLIGENCE SUMMARY.~~ 16th (Royal Devon Yeo.) Bn DEVON REGT.

(Erase heading not required.)

Army Form C. 2118.

Place	Date	Hour	Summary of Events and Information	Remarks and references to Appendices
Grammont				
"	25.2.19	9-4	do do do.	
"	26.2.19	9-4	Baths for Battalion at Grammont. Company Parades. Educational & Recreational Training.	
"	27.2.19	9-4	Company Parades. Educational & Recreational Training.	
"	28.2.19	9-4	do do do.	

1/3/19.

[signature]
Capt
~~Lt. Col.~~ Comdg. ~~Capt. & Adjutant~~
Royal Devon ~~Royal Devon Yeo. Batt~~
Devonshire Regt. ~~Devonshire Reg~~

(A9175) Wt W2358/P.66 6,0,000 12/17 D. D. & L. Sch. 52a. Forms/C2118/15

Army Form C. 2118.

Instructions regarding War Diaries and Intelligence Summaries are contained in F. S. Regs., Part II, and the Staff Manual respectively. Title pages will be prepared in manuscript.

WAR DIARY
or
~~INTELLIGENCE SUMMARY~~ 16th (Royal Devon Yeo.) Bn DEVON REGT. MARCH 1919

(Erase heading not required.)

ROYAL DEVON YEOMANRY BATTn. No. .... Date .... DEVONSHIRE REGIMENT

Vol 12

Place	Date	Hour	Summary of Events and Information	Remarks and references to Appendices
GRAMMONT. BELGIUM.	1/3/19	9-4	Company Parades. Educational & Recreational Training.	
"	2/3/19	10.45	Church Service in Battalion Billets (D. Coy). RUE DE COLLEGE. MAJOR E.J.H. HOLLEY. M.C proceeded UK on leave. CAPT. F.R. ARCHER assumed command of the Battalion.	
"	3/3/19	9-4	Company Parades. Educational & Recreational Training.	
"	4/3/19	9-4	Company Parades. Recreational Training. 5 officers & 102 Other Ranks proceeded to ETAPLES for attachment to 2/4th Oxford & Bucks Light Infantry. (Army of occupation).	
"	5/3/19	9-4	Company Parades. Recreational Training.	
"	6/3/19	9-4	do do do do	
"	7/3/19	9-4	do do do do	
"	8/3/19	9-4	do do do do	
"	9/3/19	10.00	Church Service in the Royal Highlanders Recreation Room. GRAMMONT. Lt-Col. E.J.H. HOLLEY returned from Leave U.K. & resumes command of the BATTALION.	
"	10/3/19	9-4	Company Parades. Recreational Training.	
"	11/3/19	9-4	Company Parades. Recreational Training. 39 ORs proceeded UK for demobilization.	
"	12/3/19	9-4	do do.	
	13/3/19	9-4	do do	
	14/3/19	9. 4	do do	
	15/3/19	9. 4	do do 10 ORs proceeded to UK for demobilization.	

E. J. H. Holley
Lt. Col. Comd.
Royal Devon Yeo. Batt.
Devonshire Regt.

(A9175) Wt W2358/P360 6,0,000 12/17 D. D. & L. Sch. 52a. Forms/C2118/15

Instructions regarding War Diaries and Intelligence Summaries are contained in F. S. Regs., Part II. and the Staff Manual respectively. Title pages will be prepared in manuscript.

WAR DIARY

or

~~INTELLIGENCE SUMMARY~~.

(Erase heading not required.)

Army Form C. 2118.

ROYAL DEVON YEOMANRY BATT.n 16th (Royal Devon Yeo.) Bn DEVON REGT.

Place	Date	Hour	Summary of Events and Information	Remarks and references to Appendices
GRAMMONT.	16/3/19	11 AM	Church Service in the Black Watch Hall.	
BELGUIM.	17/3/19	9-4	Company parades. Recreational Training.	
"	18/3/19	9-4 1.30pm	do do. Divisional Gymkana.	
"	19/3/19	9-12.	The Batt.n have use of Foden Lorry for blankets to be disinfected. 2-4 Recreational Training	
"	20/3/19	9-10.15 to 20 2-4	Company parades. Medical Officer's inspection Recreational Training	
"	21/3/19	9-11-30 1.30-5-30	Parades under company arrangements Battalion have the use of baths at Grammont. 1 officer & 3 OR proceed to UK for demobilization	
"	22/3/19	9-11.30	Parades under company arrangements.	
"	23/3/19	11. AM	Church service in the YMCA. Grand Place Grammont	
"	24/3/19		Battalion moves to new billeting area Grammont.	
"	25/3/19	9-4	Company parades. Recreational Training	
"	26/3/19	9.4	do do	
"	27/3/19	9-12.	Battalion have use of Foden Lorry for disinfecting blankets. 2 officers & 6 OR proceeded to UK for demobilization	
"	28/3/19	9-11.30 1.30-3.30	Parades under company arrangements Battalion have use of the baths at Grammont	
"	29/3/19	9-4.	Company parades & Recreational Training	
"	30/3/19	11.15	Church service in YMCA Grammont	
	31/3/19	9. 11.30 1.30 pm	Company parades. Divisional Gymkana.	

E. A. H. [illegible]

Royal Devon Yeo. Batt. Devonshire Regt.

(A9175) Wt W2351/P360 600,000 12/17 D. D. & L. Sch 52a Forms/C2118/15

Instructions regarding War Diaries and Intelligence Summaries are contained in F. S. Regs., Part II, and the Staff Manual respectively. Title pages will be prepared in manuscript.

WAR DIARY
or
~~INTELLIGENCE SUMMARY~~. 16th (Royal Devon Yeo.) Bn DEVON REGT.

(*Erase heading not required.*)

Army Form C. 2118.

Vol 13

Place	Date	Hour	Summary of Events and Information	Remarks and references to Appendices
GRAMMONT	1/4/19	0900	Company Parades. Afternoon Recreational Training	
"	2/4/19	0900 / 1130	" " " " " Lt Col A. C. Mardon D.S.O demobilized	
"	3/4/19	0900 / 1130	" " " Baths. 1400 Cadre inspected by C.O.	
"			Lieut Kay rejoins from draft conducting	
"	4/4/19	0900	Company Parades & recreational training	
"	5/4/19	0900	" " & recreational training. Lt R.N. Dollimore proceeds to join 1st Bn Oxford & Bucks Light Infantry Aldershot; Lt Devonshire proceeds on leave U.K.	
"	6/4/19	[illegible]	[illegible] GRAMMONT	
"	7.4.19	0900	Company Parades. – Afternoon. Recreational Training.	
			2/Lt. D.A FALCONER proceeded to D.A.D.R.E. No. 5 AREA LILLE for duty.	
"	8.4.19	0900	Company Parades. – Afternoon. Recreational Training.	
			Lt. B DENCH proceeded to 861. R.E Coy. CALAIS for duty.	
"	9.4.19	0900.	Company Parades. – Afternoon. Recreational Training.	
			Lt. L.C.R. FARNSWORTH proceeded U.K for demobilization.	
			2/Lt. L.H. GENT returned from duty at REBAIX.	

aRJl

(A9175) Wt W2353/P363 650,000 12/17 D. D. & L. Sch. 52a. Forms/C2118/15

Instructions regarding War Diaries and Intelligence Summaries are contained in F. S. Regs., Part II. and the Staff Manual respectively. Title pages will be prepared in manuscript.

WAR DIARY

or

[redacted]

16th (Royal Devon Yeo.) Bn. DEVON REGT.

(*Erase heading not required.*)

Army Form C. 2118.

Place	Date	Hour	Summary of Events and Information	Remarks and references to Appendices
GRAMMONT.	10.4.19	0900	Company Parades. Afternoon Recreational Training.	
"				
"	11.4.19	0900 / 1000	Company Parades.	
"	"	1100 / 1230	Baths at GRAMMONT. Inspection of Cadre by Commanding	Officer.
			Lt. Col. E.J.H. HOLLEY M.C. proceeded on Special Leave to U.K.	
			MAJOR F.R. ARCHER assumed Command of Battalion vice	
			Lt. Col. E.J.H. HOLLEY M.C.	
			2/Lt. CREED returned from Draft Conducting duties.	
"	12.4.19	0900	Kit Inspection by Company Commanders.	
			Afternoon Recreational Training.	
"	13.4.19	0900	Church Service in Y.M.C.A. GRAMMONT.	
"	14.4.19	0900	Company Parades. Afternoon Recreational Training.	
			1 Off. 4 O.Rs. proceeded U.K. for demobilization.	
			2/Lt. F.J. SCHRADER appointed Battalion Fire Officer.	
"	15.4.19	0900	Company Parades. Afternoon Recreational Training.	
			Lt. J.H. DAY proceeded to 214 P.O.W. Coy. PERONNE for duty.	
			2/Lts. D.H. GENT & L.J. HANSON proceeded to 213 P.O.W. Coy. QUENAST	for duty.

aRfl

(A9173) Wt W2153/P160 650,000 12/17 D. D. & L. Sch. 52a. Forms/C2118/15.

Instructions regarding War Diaries and Intelligence Summaries are contained in F. S. Regs., Part II. and the Staff Manual respectively. Title pages will be prepared in manuscript.

WAR DIARY

or

~~INTELLIGENCE SUMMARY~~ 6th (Royal Devon Yeo.) Bn DEVON REGT.

(Erase heading not required.)

Army Form C. 2118.

Place	Date	Hour	Summary of Events and Information	Remarks and references to Appendices
GRAMMONT	16.4.19	0900	Company Parades. Recreational Training.	
			Inspection of ORs. for Army of Occupation by Commanding Officer.	
"	17.4.19	0900	Company Parades. Recreational Training.	
"	"	0400	60 O.Rs. proceeded to ETAPLES in charge of 2/Lt. H. BROWN	
			to join 2/4th OXFORD & BUCKS L.I. for Army of Occupation.	
"	18.4.19	0900	GOOD FRIDAY - HOLIDAY.	
"	19.4.19	0900	General Parade. [illegible] for [illegible]	
"	20.4.19	0900	[illegible]	
			[illegible]	
	[illegible] 19	[illegible]	[illegible] Holiday.	
"	22.4.19	0900	General Parade. Cricket & Baseball Match.	
"	23.4.19	0900	[illegible] Cricket Match in the afternoon.	
"	24.4.19	0900	General Parade. Inspection of Transport by the Divisional Commander.	
"	"	1400	[illegible] Match.	
"	25.4.19	0900	General Parade. [illegible] of [illegible] Sports [illegible] during afternoon.	
"	26.4.19	0900	General Parade.	

arpl

Instructions regarding War Diaries and Intelligence Summaries are contained in F. S. Regs., Part II. and the Staff Manual respectively. Title pages will be prepared in manuscript.

WAR DIARY

or

~~INTELLIGENCE SUMMARY~~.

(Erase heading not required.)

Army Form C. 2118.

ROYAL DEVON YEOMANRY BATT[N] * DEVONSHIRE REGIMENT Date.............

Place	Date	Hour	Summary of Events and Information	Remarks and references to Appendices
GRAMMONT.	27.4.19	0900	General Routine. & Church Service in Y.M.C.A	
"	28.4.19	0900	General Routine. Inspection of Billets by Commanding Officer.	
"	"	11.30	[illegible] run off in Brigade Sports at Grammont.	
"	29.4.19	0900	General Routine. Inspection of Harness by Commanding Officer.	
"	30.4.19	0900	General Routine.	

A.R. [illegible] Capt.
for Major ~~Lt. Col.~~ Comg.
Royal Devon Yeo. Batt.
Devonshire Regt.

1/1919.

D. D. & L., London, E.C.
(A8031) Wt. W1771/M2031 750,000 5/17 **Sch. 52** Forms C2118/14

Army Form C. 2118.

Instructions regarding War Diaries and Intelligence Summaries are contained in F. S. Regs., Part II. and the Staff Manual respectively. Title pages will be prepared in manuscript.

WAR DIARY
or
~~INTELLIGENCE SUMMARY~~ 16th (Royal Devon Yeo.) Bn DEVON REGT.
(Erase heading not required.)

18 14

Place	Date	Hour	Summary of Events and Information	Remarks and references to Appendices
[illegible]	[illegible]		[illegible] Lt. Col. [illegible] M.C. returned from [illegible]	
			[illegible] command of the Batt[illegible]	
			[illegible] ARCHER and [illegible] C. Devonshire M.C.	
			[illegible] to KEBAN for duty at CORCOL C.	
			[illegible]	
			[illegible]	
			[illegible] proceeded to WATERLOO and	
			[illegible]	
			[illegible] LOUVAIN [illegible]	
			[illegible]	
			[illegible]	
			[illegible]	
			[illegible]	MH

(A9175) Wt W2355/P561 600,000 12/17 D. D. & L. Sch. 52a. Forms/C2118/15

Instructions regarding War Diaries and Intelligence Summaries are contained in F. S. Regs., Part II, and the Staff Manual respectively. Title pages will be prepared in manuscript.

WAR DIARY

or

~~INTELLIGENCE SUMMARY~~. 16th (Royal Devon Yeo.) Bn DEVON REGT.

(Erase heading not required.)

Army Form C. 2118.

Place	Date	Hour	Summary of Events and Information	Remarks and references to Appendices
Grammont	[illegible]/5/19	0900	General Routine.	
"	11/5/19	0900	General Routine.	
"	12/5/19	0900	General Routine & Baths at GRAMMONT.	
"	[illegible]/5/19	0900	General Routine.	
"	[illegible]/5/19	0900	General Routine. 1 OR proceeded UK on Special leave.	
"	15/5/19	0900	General Routine. 3 Officers & 12 ORs under [illegible] Bruges [illegible] & returned to [illegible].	
"	[illegible]/5/19	0900	General Routine. 1 OR proceeded UK for repatriation to Canada.	
	[illegible]	[illegible]	General Routine. 1 OR proceeded UK for repatriation to U.S.A.	
	[illegible]	[illegible]	[illegible] Routine	
	[illegible]	[illegible]	[illegible] Routine	
	[illegible]	[illegible]	General Routine.	
	[illegible]	[illegible]	General Routine	
	[illegible]	[illegible]	General Routine	
	[illegible]/5/19	0900	General Routine	
	[illegible]/5/19	0900	General Routine. 1 OR returned from leave in U.K.	
	[illegible]/5/19	0900	General Routine. 2/Lt C. REED proceeded U.K. for demobilization.	

N.R.

Instructions regarding War Diaries and Intelligence Summaries are contained in F. S. Regs., Part II. and the Staff Manual respectively. Title pages will be prepared in manuscript.

WAR DIARY
or
~~INTELLIGENCE SUMMARY.~~
(Erase heading not required.)

Army Form C. 2118.

16th (Royal Devon Yeo.) Bn DEVON REGT.

Place	Date	Hour	Summary of Events and Information	Remarks and references to Appendices
[illegible]	26-5-19	0900	General Routine. 1 O.R. proceeded to 2/4 Ox & Bucks L.I. 2 O.R. proceeded to U.K. for 14 days Ordinary Leave. Lt. Col. E.J.H. HOLLEY. M.C. proceeded to U.K. on Special Leave.	
"	27-5-19	0900	General Routine	
"	28-5-19	0900	General Routine Capt & Adjt. A.R.J. CYSTER proceeded to U.K. for 14 days Ordinary Leave	
"	29-5-19	0900	General Routine.	
"	30-5-19	0900	General Routine	
"	31-5-19	0900	General Routine S/Lt. F. J. SCHRADER proceeded to U.K. for Repatriation	

R. F. Mackay Capt. ~~Lt. Col.~~ Comg.
Royal Devon Yeo. Batt.
Devonshire Regt.

(A9175) W: W2358/P363 600,000 12/17 D. D. & L. Sch. 52a. Forms/C2118/15

H.Q.

3 Inf Bde

Herewith original War Diary of this unit for month past. Kindly [illegible] please.

1.7.16

A.H. [illegible]

Lt Adjt

16 Bn

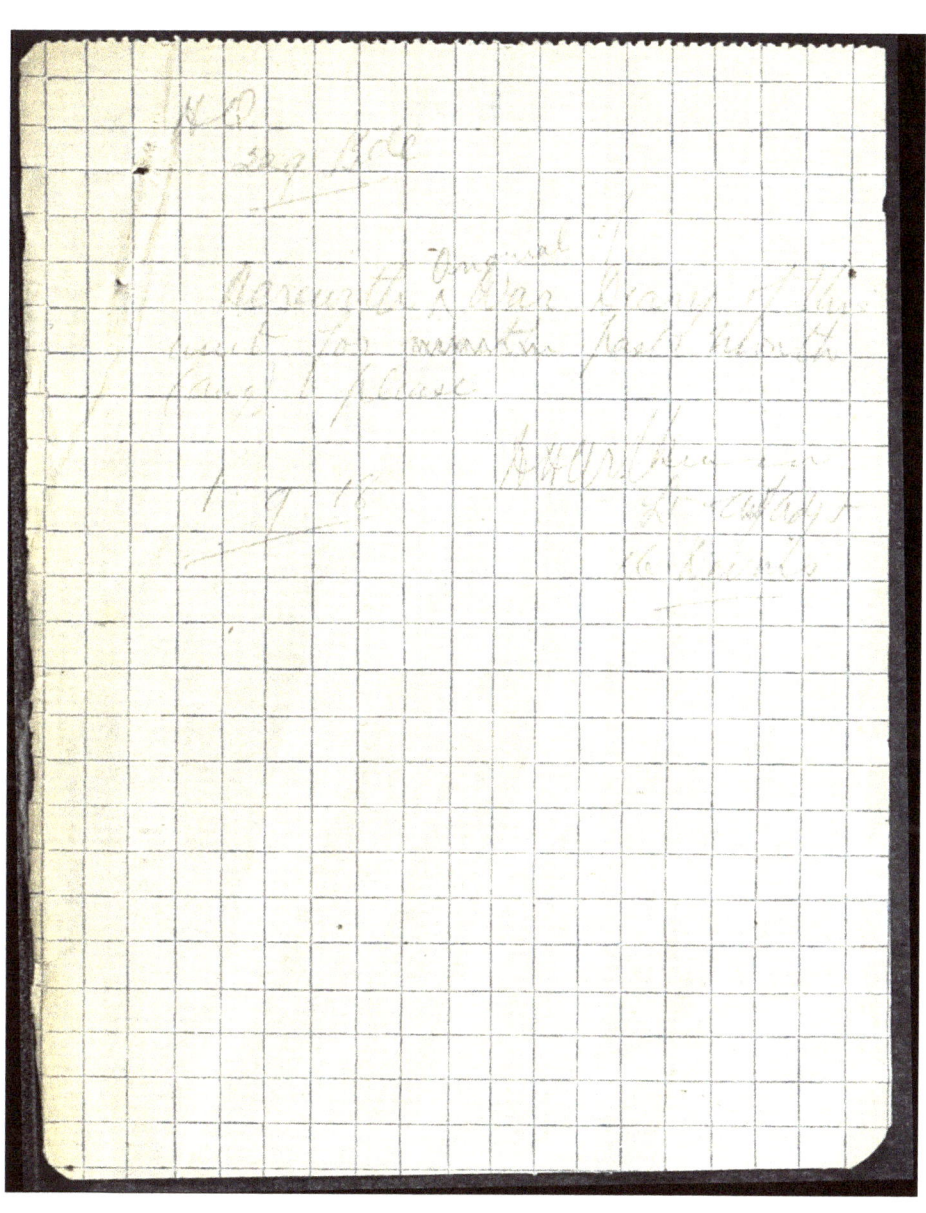

www.ingramcontent.com/pod-product-compliance
Lightning Source LLC
Chambersburg PA
CBHW081454160426
43193CB00013B/2478